# VULTURES

LIVING WILD

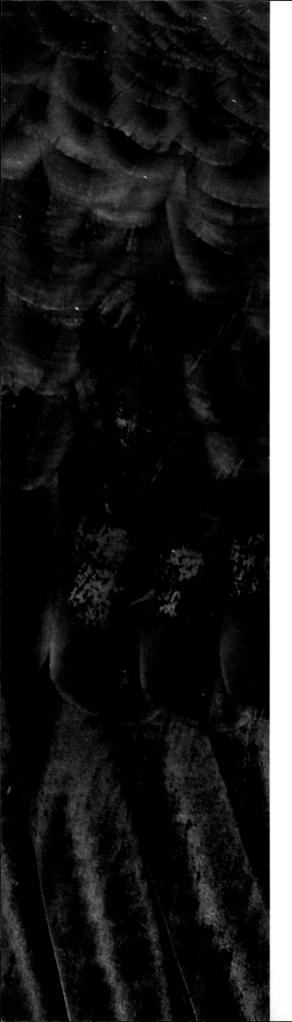

# LIVING WILD

Published by Creative Education
P.O. Box 227, Mankato, Minnesota 56002
Creative Education is an imprint of The Creative Company
www.thecreativecompany.us

Design and production by Mary Herrmann
Art direction by Rita Marshall
Printed in the United States of America

Photographs by Alamy (JJM Stock Photography, Luc Novovitch, Chetan Rangaraj, Emmanuel Rondeau), Dreamstime (Paul Banton, Basphoto, Bpperry, Evajoy, Anton Foltin, Franky, Juan Pablo Fuentes Serrano, Hans232, Neil Harrison, Hdanne, Holger Karius, Lijuan Guo, Lukas Maton, Stephen Meese, Derrick Neill, Netfalls, Amy Nicolai, Oksanaphoto, Tanja Pals, South12th, Stefanov764, Graham Taylor, Karin Van Ijzendoorn, Peter Wey, Paul Wolf, Kim Worrell), Getty Images (Gerry Ellis, Win McNamee, Tom Vezo), iStockphoto (Judith Bicking, Waltraud Ingerl, David Kerkhoff, Tobias Müller, Graeme Purdy, Berndt Vorwold), Shutterstock (Nick Biemans, Nazzu, Janet Quantrill, Nickolay Stanev)

Library of Congress Cataloging-in-Publication Data
Gish, Melissa.
Vultures / by Melissa Gish.
p. cm. — (Living wild)
Includes bibliographical references and index.
Summary: A look at vultures, including their habitats, physical characteristics such as their bald heads, behaviors, relationships with humans, and persecuted status in the world today.
ISBN 978-1-60818-171-1
1. Vultures—Juvenile literature. I. Title.

QL696.F32G575 2012
598.9'4—dc23    2011035795

First Edition
9 8 7 6 5 4 3 2 1

**CREATIVE EDUCATION**

# VULTURES

Melissa Gish

It is late July in southern Arizona's Saguaro National Park, and the scorching

sun bakes the rocky earth. Four turkey
vultures circle in the cloudless sky.

It is late July in southern Arizona's Saguaro National Park, and the scorching sun bakes the rocky earth. Four turkey vultures circle in the cloudless sky, scanning a landscape dotted with prickly creosote shrubs; slender, spiked ocotillo; tall saguaro cacti; and dozens of other desert plants. Suddenly, a scent catches the vultures' attention. They flap their wings to change direction and begin descending. More than a mile (1.6 km) below is the source of the

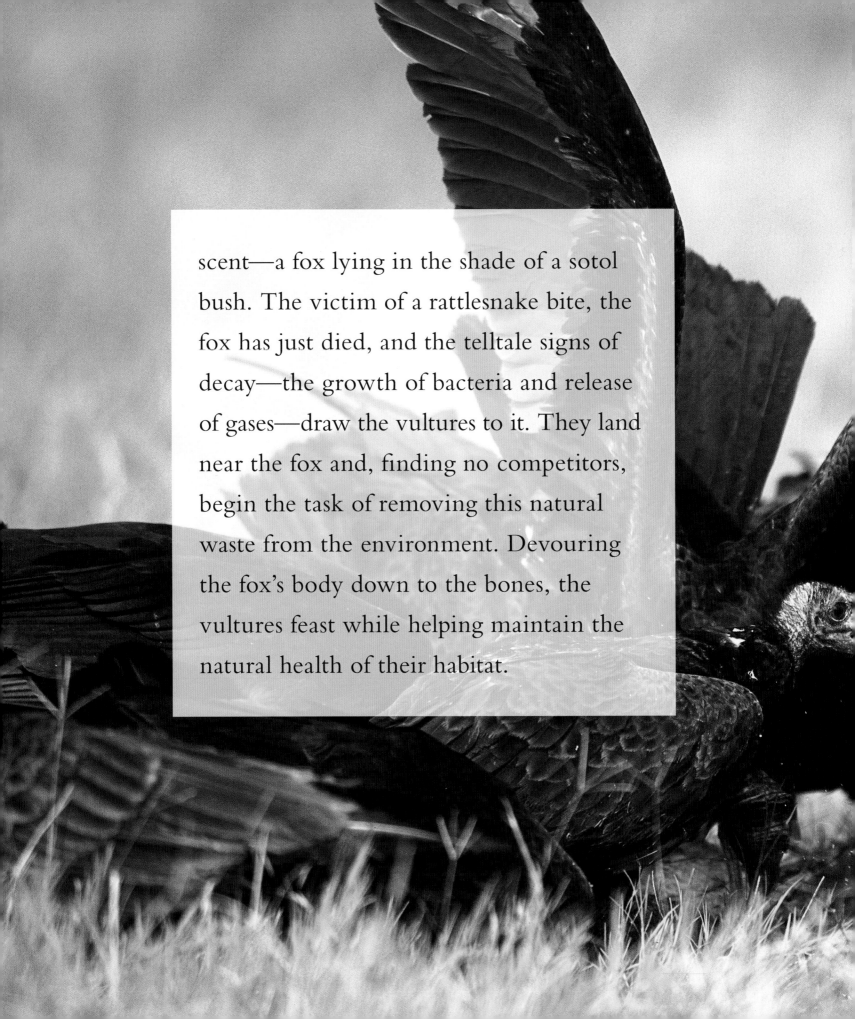

scent—a fox lying in the shade of a sotol bush. The victim of a rattlesnake bite, the fox has just died, and the telltale signs of decay—the growth of bacteria and release of gases—draw the vultures to it. They land near the fox and, finding no competitors, begin the task of removing this natural waste from the environment. Devouring the fox's body down to the bones, the vultures feast while helping maintain the natural health of their habitat.

# WHERE IN THE WORLD THEY LIVE

■ **Turkey Vulture**
throughout
the Americas

□ **Cinereous Vulture**
southern Europe
and Asia

■ **Lappet-faced
Vulture**
Africa

□ **Andean Condor**
western coast of
South America

■ **Indian Vulture**
Pakistan and India

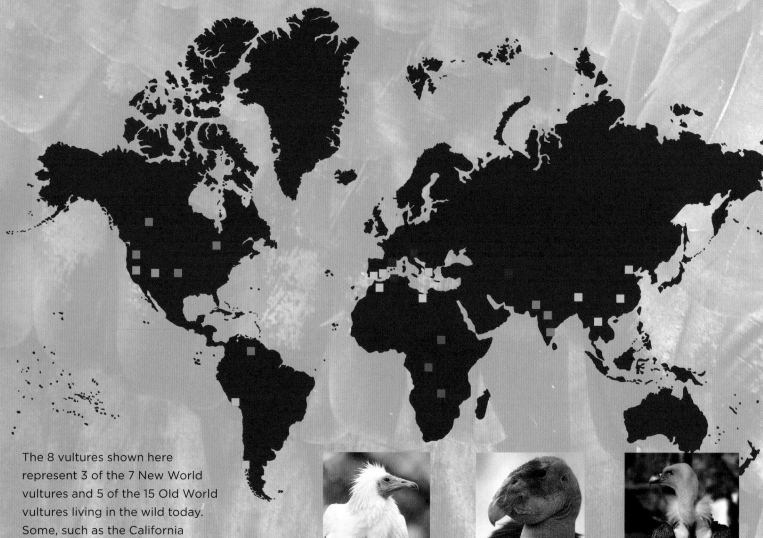

The 8 vultures shown here represent 3 of the 7 New World vultures and 5 of the 15 Old World vultures living in the wild today. Some, such as the California condor, number only in the hundreds and are confined to small parcels of land, while others, such as the turkey vulture, number in the millions and range over vast expanses of territory.

**Egyptian Vulture**
southwestern Europe
and northern Africa
to southern Asia

■ **California Condor**
Arizona, west-
central California

■ **Griffon Vulture**
southern Europe,
Asia, North Africa

## EATERS OF THE DEAD

Vultures are found on all but two of Earth's continents—Antarctica and Australia—and everywhere vultures are found, people have traditionally viewed them as messengers of death. The name "vulture" originally comes from the Latin word *vultur*, which is related to another word for "tearing," and is associated with the manner in which vultures feed—by tearing at the flesh of animals. Vultures are sometimes called buzzards, but buzzards are members of a different genus.

The 22 different species of vulture, in the order Falconiformes, are divided into 2 groups: Old World vultures and New World vultures. The 15 species of Eurasian and African Old World vulture, in the family Accipitridae, include the Egyptian and hooded vultures as well as Cape griffons. The New World vultures, in the family Cathartidae, are found in the Americas. This group includes the most widespread species, the turkey vulture, as well as the rarest, the California condor.

As birds, vultures are **warm-blooded**, feathered, beaked animals that walk on two feet and lay eggs. Vultures are also raptors, or birds of prey. As scavengers, they descend

*The California condor, the largest bird in North America, has a wingspan of more than 10 feet (3 m).*

**Observers in India reported that six to eight vultures can clean a butchered cow carcass down to bare bones in about one hour.**

on dying or dead animals and use their hooked beaks to tear apart flesh. Lacking an avian syrinx, the organ in birds that produces song, New World vultures are usually silent except while feeding, when they may fight with other vultures and make hissing and coughing sounds. While the two groups of vultures resemble each other physically, Old World vultures are more closely related to other raptors—hawks, harriers, buzzards, kites, and eagles—than to New World vultures. Vultures look most like eagles except for the lack of feathers on their heads. This is an important characteristic for vultures, which often have their beaks buried in decaying flesh and would thus have trouble keeping a feathered face clean.

A vulture's beak is covered with keratin, the same material found in human fingernails, and it grows continuously. Normal use of the beak keeps it both sharp and worn down to an appropriate length. A hungry vulture is an efficient eater. Its hooked beak rips into **carrion**, tearing flesh to pieces. Then, using the sharp edges of its beak like knives, the vulture slices off pieces of flesh and swallows the meat whole. Vultures have enormous appetites and can eat up to 20 percent of their

*The pink or reddish color of a lappet-faced vulture's head is a distinctive mark of this Old World species.*

*King vultures, among the largest New World vultures, are found in tropical forests from southern Mexico to Argentina.*

body weight in one sitting. Some vultures devour entire carcasses—fur, bones, and all.

The New World king vulture of Central and South America is one of the most colorful vultures. Its head and beak may include varying colors of red, orange, yellow, blue, and purple. The Andean condor, named for its habitat in the Andes Mountains, has a striking white ruffle of feathers around its neck. At 10.5 feet (3.2 m), this vulture has the largest wingspan of any land bird. Perhaps the most familiar Old World vulture is the lappet-faced of northern Africa. It is an aggressive bird that may chase other vultures away from a food source and even attack small prey—an unusual behavior for scavenging vultures. The white-headed vulture of Africa sports a pink beak, and the critically endangered red-headed vulture of northern India and Nepal has red, fleshy flaps on either side of its neck.

Like their ancestors, modern birds have hollow bones, making them lightweight for flight. Male vultures are typically about 10 percent larger than females, but in some vulture species, the characteristic is reversed. Vultures have powerful wings that are long and wide, which enables them to glide for great distances without

*Northern India's Ranthambore National Park provides a safe haven for red-headed vultures to roam.*

*Vultures get most of the moisture they need from the meat they eat, but they drink water when they can find it.*

flapping. Some species, such as the American black vulture, have short wings, requiring them to flap more often than other vultures but also allowing them to maneuver through their forested habitat with greater ease. In open spaces, vultures ride upward-moving currents of warm air. These circular currents are called thermals. By riding thermals, vultures can soar for hours without once flapping their wings and are thus often seen circling rather than soaring in a straight line.

With a wingspan of 10 feet (3 m) and a weight of up to 31 pounds (14 kg), the Old World cinereous (*sih-NIH-ree-us*) vulture is one of the largest and heaviest of the world's birds of prey. It is found across southern Europe and Asia. Due to habitat destruction, it is no longer as plentiful in Europe as it once was and is considered a near-threatened species. One of the rarest birds of prey in Europe, the lammergeier (*LAM-er-geer*), also known as the bearded vulture, has an equally impressive wingspan of 10 feet (3 m), but it weighs only up to 17 pounds (7.7 kg). This bird is dubbed "the bone breaker" because it drops large bones from great heights in order to shatter them to expose the soft, edible marrow inside.

**The Cherokee American Indians call the turkey vulture the "peace eagle" because this bird does not kill its prey.**

Old World vultures have strong legs and sharp talons for seizing and carrying chunks of meat away from competitors such as hyenas. Since New World vultures rarely compete with land animals for prey that is already dead, these birds **evolved** differently. Their short legs and chicken-like feet are designed for standing rather than for carrying animals. All vultures have three toes that point forward and one that points backward. Like the beak, talons are made of keratin and grow throughout a vulture's life. Clawing on the bones of carrion, running on the ground, and clutching tree branches and other perches keep vultures' talons from growing too long.

To find food, Old World vultures rely on their powerful vision. A vulture's eyes are located on the sides of its skull. Vultures look outward and forward at the same time. This is called binocular vision, and it helps vultures judge distances precisely. The eye of a vulture has a see-through inner eyelid called a nictitating (*NIK-tih-tayt-ing*) membrane that closes from front to back, wiping dust from the eyeball and shielding the sensitive **pupil** from direct sunlight. Vultures have poor night vision and thus seek food only during the day. New World vultures

also have good daytime eyesight, but they rely mainly on their keen sense of smell to locate food. Circling high above the ground, these vultures can detect even the slightest traces of ethyl mercaptan, an odorous gas produced by decaying flesh, within about 12 hours of an animal's death.

*While most birds have relatively poor vision as compared with humans, vultures can see just as far as we can.*

*During mating season, a solitary vulture may glide through an area for hours, searching for a suitable mate.*

## RIDING THE WIND

M ost species of vulture can live up to 25 years in the wild and more than 30 years in captivity. The oldest captive vulture is Toulouse, a turkey vulture, which arrived at Marine World in Redwood City, California, as an orphaned fledgling in 1972. As of 2012, he was still in good health at his home in the San Francisco Zoo.

Vultures reach maturity and are ready to mate at three to four years of age. Most vulture species remain with a single mate for life, but if one dies, the other will find a new mate. To choose a mate, vultures perform various courtship rituals. Turkey vultures participate in a particularly unique courtship behavior called the group dance. A small group of vultures gathers on the ground, and the birds stretch out their wings. The dance begins when one bird lowers its head and hops toward a second bird. Then the second bird lowers its head and hops toward a third. This pattern continues, with more birds joining the dance, until all the birds finally break away in pairs.

The king vulture dances, too, but it does so only with its selected partner. Two king vultures stretch out their

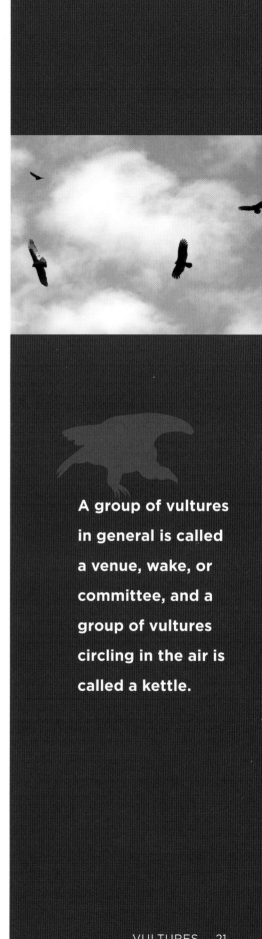

A group of vultures in general is called a venue, wake, or committee, and a group of vultures circling in the air is called a kettle.

*Only Old World vultures build nests in tall trees and defend their young from this high vantage point.*

wings, lower their heads, and circle each other while flapping their wings and making wheezing sounds. Only the lammergeier participates in aerial acrobatics similar to those conducted by eagles. A pair of lammergeiers flies around a selected nesting site, then soars high into the air—up to 10,000 feet (3,048 m)—at which point they lock talons, then fall, spinning cartwheels in the air. They break apart at the last moment and fly back up into the sky.

While dances and flight displays serve to impress vulture mates, the behavior that secures the bond between two vultures is nesting. Old World vulture partners build nests from twigs and branches on the ground, on cliff ledges, or in treetops. New World vultures do not build nests like those of other birds. Instead, they settle in secluded spots on the ground, in tree hollows, or in abandoned buildings.

With the exception of the Andean condor, which lays a single egg every other year, female vultures annually lay one to three eggs at a rate of one egg per day. The eggs are three to five inches (7.6–12.7 cm) long, depending on the species, and vary in color from dull white to speckled brown. A group of eggs is called a clutch.

Like all birds' eggs, vulture eggs must be incubated, or kept warm, while the baby vultures are developing inside. Both parents take turns sitting in the nest with the eggs situated under the breast and wings. Vultures incubate their eggs from 30 to 70 days, or until the baby vultures, called chicks, hatch.

Using its **egg tooth**, the chick breaks through the hard shell of its egg. This may take between 12 and 48 hours. Most newly hatched chicks weigh less than six ounces (170 g), and all chicks can immediately eat food that their mothers share with them. The mother stores food in her crop, a pouch in her throat, and brings the food up again,

*The lammergeier is peculiar among vultures for many reasons, not the least of which is its feathered head.*

A lammergeier has one or two offspring a year and nests on a cliff ledge to keep its chicks away from predators.

either directly into her chick's mouth or into the nest where the chick can reach it. Vultures are weak at first and crawl around the nest on their knees, which are called shanks. As they grow bigger, vulture chicks often fight over food, and in many cases, the first-hatched chick will kill its younger siblings in a practice called siblicide. This survival instinct enables the remaining chick to benefit from being the sole recipient of all food.

Vultures are born with light gray or white down and white or gray faces. The soft down grows darker and thicker over the first several weeks of a vulture's life. Depending on the mature coloration of the species, the chick's face changes color to black, gray, brown, pink, or red. By the time most vultures are two to three months old, feathers have replaced their down, and they can flap their wings, lifting themselves off the nest floor. As it gains strength, a vulture may leave the nest to explore its surroundings, but it will depend on its parents for food for at least another month or two. Smaller vulture species grow, learn to fly, and leave the nest within three to four months. Larger vulture species, such as Andean and California condors, remain with their parents for five to

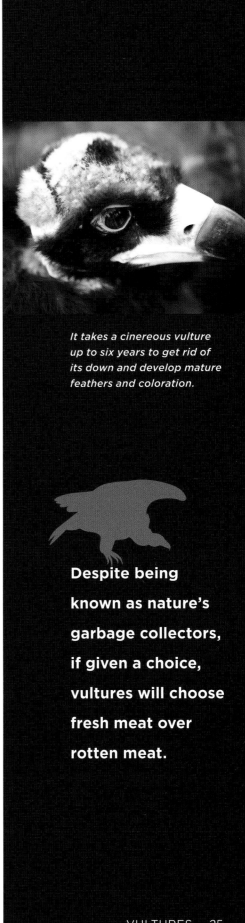

*It takes a cinereous vulture up to six years to get rid of its down and develop mature feathers and coloration.*

**Despite being known as nature's garbage collectors, if given a choice, vultures will choose fresh meat over rotten meat.**

seven months before they are fully feathered and ready to fly, and they may continue to receive food from their parents for an additional five months. When a juvenile vulture leaves the nest, it will have to compete with other vultures for food. Depending on the species, a juvenile may not yet have its adult **plumage** at that time. For example, the white feathers on the palm-nut vulture's body remain brown until this bird is three or four years old.

As a detrivore (an animal that eats the dead remains of other animals), the vulture helps maintain a healthy environment for all living things in its habitat. Vultures aid in the natural cycle of decay and also help reduce the spread of animal illnesses. Possessing a powerful stomach acid that can resist many types of bacterial and viral infections, vultures are able to clean up diseased carrion that would be harmful to other animals. In addition, the vulture's digestive system contains its own bacteria that kill most harmful microorganisms, and as a result, the bird's droppings are free of disease. In addition, antibacterial properties in a vulture's urine, which is released onto the bird's legs, help it serve as a natural cleanser after the bird walks over diseased carrion.

Adult vultures have few natural enemies. Juveniles may fall prey to large eagles, and vultures engaged in a group feeding may suffer attacks from other scavengers, such as hyenas in Africa and coyotes in North America. These animals will steal food from vultures and sometimes even kill them. Human destruction of vulture habitat and the shooting, trapping, and poisoning of vultures have dramatically reduced the numbers of many vulture species—including seven of the nine species inhabiting South Africa.

*Hyenas, like vultures, are often thought of as scavenging animals, but they kill about 95 percent of their food.*

In 2011, a GPS-wearing vulture was captured in Saudi Arabia and accused of being a spy for Israel.

## NOBLE SCAVENGERS

N o other bird in history has been so alternately revered and detested as the vulture. Considered by many to be the living image of death and decay, the vulture is also a symbol of cleansing and rebirth. South Africa's tiny O. R. Tambo District Municipality took the latter view when it adopted a **coat of arms** in 2001 that includes a vulture as a symbol of the area's efforts to clean up crime, poverty, and disease among its people. The New World vulture genus *Cathartes*—composed of the turkey, lesser yellow-headed, and greater yellow-headed vultures—takes its name from the Greek word *katharsis*, meaning "cleansing." However, many vulture species are today considered pests because they can crash into airplanes, destroy rooftops, and litter public places with feces and carrion. Because all birds of prey in America are protected from poisoning, shooting, and similar forms of control under the Migratory Bird Act of 1918, sound devices are typically used to scare away unwanted birds. In other parts of the world, however, vultures have been violently persecuted.

Artifacts—some nearly 12,000 years old—that show

To meet their nutritional needs, vultures prefer to eat herbivores, or plant-eating animals, rather than carnivores, or meat-eating animals.

**One of the few bird species to use tools, an Egyptian vulture teaches its young to use rocks to crack open ostrich eggs.**

vultures being used as cultural symbols have been discovered in the Middle East. In Turkey in 1958, British archaeologist James Mellaart found the **Neolithic** city of Çatalhöyük, dating back to 7500 B.C., and American archaeologists Ralph and Rose Solecki began excavating the village of Zawi Chemi Shanidar, dating back to 9800 B.C. In both cities, paintings were discovered on the interior walls of buildings that depicted enormous vultures and headless humans. Also discovered were wing bones and feathers from griffon vultures and lammergeiers, which scholars believe were used in rituals and costumes. When Eannatum, a ruler in the region of Sumer (present-day Iraq), conquered a neighboring kingdom in about 2500 B.C., he erected a stone monument, called a stele, carved with images of his victory. Now housed in the Louvre Museum in Paris, fragments of the "Stele of the Vultures" show hordes of vultures descending upon a battlefield.

Ancient Egyptians used vultures to symbolize the protective nature of motherhood. Nekhbet, the goddess of Upper Egypt and the symbol of birth and motherhood, is often depicted as a vulture holding an ankh, the symbol of eternal life, and sometimes with her wings

spread to symbolize her protection of the pharaoh. Conversely, Nekhbet's sister Wadjet, the cobra, was the goddess of Lower Egypt and the symbol of death. As Egyptian beliefs evolved, Mut, the great mother goddess of Egypt, emerged. She wore a feathered gown and a vulture headdress. As time passed, Mut was revered as a grandmotherly figure, and her daughter Isis became the new mother goddess. Isis is often shown wearing a vulture on her crown in reference to Mut. Real-life Egyptian

*Nekhbet was depicted as carrying either an ankh or a shen ring (shown), the symbol of eternal protection.*

*Egyptian hieroglyphs depict Mut embracing pharaohs, or kings, to express Mut's protection over them.*

queens such as Nefertari, wife of Ramses II, also wore vulture headdresses as physical reminders of their spiritual connection to the mother goddesses.

According to ancient Roman **mythology**, Romulus and Remus, the founders of Rome, were associated with vultures. In deciding where to build a new city, the men stood on two hilltops awaiting a sign from the gods. From one hill, Remus saw 6 vultures, and from the other hill, Romulus saw 12 vultures. Their followers decided that the larger group of vultures signaled that the city should be built on Romulus' hill. They named the city Rome and crowned Romulus their king.

The vulture is an important symbol among numerous **indigenous** peoples of the world, from North and South America to Africa and Asia. Many consider it to be a protector and the purifier of the world, so vulture feathers are used as symbols of cleansing and rebirth. Vulture images have appeared on headdresses, jewelry, costumes, and artwork in hundreds of cultures. Not all images are positive, however. A traditional dance of Nicaragua, called *baile del zopilote*, or the vulture dance, is performed at the burial of a bad person.

In the tradition of the Yoruba people of Nigeria and other West African countries, the vulture is a heroic figure. One story tells how the god Olodumare became angry with the other gods and goddesses, collectively called the Orisha, and forced a drought upon the land. To save their dying world, the Orisha had to beg Olodumare's forgiveness, but he lived in a distant palace near the sun, and many of the Orisha tried and failed to reach Olodumare. Finally, Ibu Kole, the most beautiful Orisha—a bird with bright plumage—made the flight. Though she struggled, and though the sun burned her feathers and scalded her head, she reached Olodumare and begged his forgiveness for the disobedience of the Orisha. Olodumare relieved the world of the drought, but Ibu Kole remained a tattered-looking, bald-headed bird—the vulture—forever.

In popular culture, Beaky Buzzard, who looks more like an Andean condor (thanks to the ruffle of white feathers around his neck), has been part of Warner Brothers' cartoons since 1942. Beaky has starred in numerous classic episodes of *Merrie Melodies* and *Looney Tunes* as well as more contemporary *Tiny Toons Adventures* and *Sylvester and Tweety*

Some scientists believe turkey vultures purposely lead coyotes to carcasses so the coyotes can open the tough hides for them.

## FROM "THE GHOSTS"

Never stoops the soaring vulture

On his quarry in the desert,

On the sick or wounded bison,

But another vulture, watching

From his high aerial look-out,

Sees the downward plunge, and follows;

And a third pursues the second,

Coming from the invisible ether,

First a speck, and then a vulture,

Till the air is dark with pinions.

So disasters come not singly;

But as if they watched and waited,

Scanning one another's motions,

When the first descends, the others

Follow, follow, gathering flock-wise

Round their victim, sick and wounded,

First a shadow, then a sorrow,

Till the air is dark with anguish.

*by Henry Wadsworth Longfellow (1807–82)*

*Mysteries* cartoons. He also had a role in the 1996 film *Space Jam*, playing basketball with star Michael Jordan.

Another animated vulture is Buzz Buzzard, who also resembles the Andean condor. Buzz, a creation of Walter Lantz Productions, first appeared with Woody Woodpecker in 1948. Since then, he has starred in dozens of cartoons, and, most recently, in two Woody Woodpecker video games and as a regular on *The New Woody Woodpecker Show.*

In the Marvel Comics universe, six different characters share the name Vulture. The most popular Vulture first appeared in 1963 as an enemy of Spider-Man whose real identity was known to be electronics engineer Adrian Toomes. He continued to wreak havoc for Spider-Man on the animated *Spider-Man* television series and in numerous Spider-Man video games. Because of the vulture's persistently negative reputation, there are virtually no heroic vulture characters in popular culture. Even in literature, vultures are usually depicted as shadowy creatures and associated with death, as in American Henry Wadsworth Longfellow's poem "The Ghosts," part of a longer work titled *The Song of Hiawatha.*

*A vulture, seemingly symbolizing death once again, is featured in this bronze sculpture related to a hanging in Mantua, Italy.*

The Painted Hills Unit, part of the John Day Fossil Beds National Monument, is an area rich in fossils.

## SURVIVAL IN A CHANGING WORLD

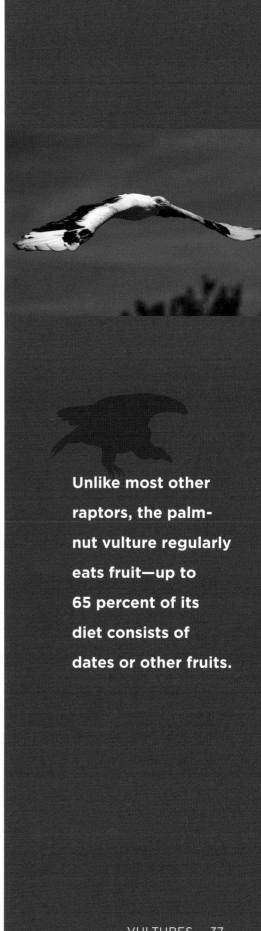

Fossil records indicate that the first raptors appeared about 50 million years ago, and scientists believe these birds may have been most closely related to New World vultures. While eagles and hawks have a rich fossil history, vulture fossils are rare and widely scattered. In Europe, vulture fossils date back only about one million years. In North America, though, a direct ancestor has been found to have lived about 2.5 to 3.5 million years ago. Named for the location of its fossil discovery in Kern County, California, the Kern vulture had a wingspan of seven to nine feet (2.1–2.7 m). Numerous fossils of an early black vulture have been found in the Fossil Lake area of Oregon as well. This bird, which lived about 11,000 years ago, was only slightly larger than modern black vultures. However, a few enormous prehistoric vulture relatives known as teratorns, or monster birds, have also been identified, some from the John Day Fossil Beds National Monument, north of Fossil Lake. The largest species, *Argentavis magnificens*, weighed more than 155 pounds (70 kg) and had a wingspan greater than 20 feet (6 m).

Unlike most other raptors, the palm-nut vulture regularly eats fruit—up to 65 percent of its diet consists of dates or other fruits.

When vultures appear to be fighting over food, they are actually cooperatively tearing carrion apart for easier feeding.

While many vulture species are plentiful today, some, such as the Indian white-rumped vulture, are dangerously close to **extinction**. Once the most abundant vulture species in India, this and two other vulture species have declined by 99 percent since 1996. Despite intense research efforts to halt the decline, scientists speculate that the Indian white-rumped vulture could become extinct by 2015. The slender-billed and Indian vultures could follow shortly thereafter. The culprit is diclofenac, a drug used to treat cattle for pain and fever. When vultures eat carrion **contaminated** with this drug, their kidneys fail, and the birds suffer a slow, painful death.

The recent discovery of diclofenac's devastating effect on vultures sparked worldwide concern for the crisis, and numerous research organizations and conservation groups made vulture research—and the banning of diclofenac—a top priority. Despite now being outlawed in India, Nepal, and Pakistan, the drug is still used illegally by thousands of farmers. A new drug, ketoprofen, has been adopted to replace diclofenac, but it affects vultures in the same way.

The continued loss of vultures in Asia has far-reaching implications. In Asia, the unused body parts of butchered cattle are routinely taken to carcass dumps. Vultures convene at these dumps and clean the meat from the bones, which then bake in the sun. Today, more cattle are raised domestically, which means there are many more carcasses in need of disposal. With vultures dying from eating the meat at these dumps, wild dogs, unaffected by diclofenac, are left to do the cleanup. But unlike vultures, whose stomach acid purifies diseased meat, wild dogs simply spread the dangerous bacteria and viruses. As the number of wild dogs has climbed in Asian farm communities, so has the spread of diseases such as anthrax and rabies. Sixty percent of all human cases of rabies now occur in India, and 96 percent of those rabies infections are caused by dog bites. Conservationists and government healthcare officials alike are desperate to bring vultures back to India and other parts of Asia.

Vultures in Africa have recently been affected by diclofenac, too. The Mankwe Wildlife Reserve in South Africa took steps to protect its vultures from diclofenac contamination by establishing a "vulture restaurant"—an area that is supplied with disease-free carcasses upon which vultures can safely feed. Vultures that visit the site are

*After lowering their body temperature at night to save energy, vultures spread their wings to warm in the morning sun.*

*About 60 percent of captive-reared California condors released into the wild survive to adulthood.*

captured and fitted with identification tags on their wings to help researchers keep track of the individuals dining at the site. Some African white-backed vultures are also fitted with small, lightweight **Global Positioning System** (GPS) devices. The weatherproof pack sits in the middle of the vulture's back between its wings. The transmitter inside the pack sends out a signal every 10 days, and a **satellite** picks up the signal and e-mails it to researchers. This information helps them locate breeding colonies and foraging ranges.

A vulture crisis struck America in the 20th century. Habitat destruction, poaching, and lead poisoning—a result of eating carcasses riddled with lead shotgun pellets—nearly wiped out the California condor. Only 22 remained in the wild in 1982, when the United States government initiated a **captive-rearing** program in cooperation with the San Diego Zoo's Wild Animal Park and the Los Angeles Zoo. Since the early 1990s, the successful program has released nearly 200 condors into the wild.

Despite being legally protected from hunting by the Migratory Bird Act of 1918, vultures in North America have been continually hunted, trapped, and poisoned because some farmers and ranchers consider them to

be **nuisance** animals. Recently, however, widespread education on the ecological value of vultures—sparked by the vulture crisis in Asia—has led to increased research and conservation efforts in the Americas. In 2003, Hawk Mountain Sanctuary in Pennsylvania started the Turkey Vulture Migration Project to learn more about the causes and effects of this bird's seasonal journeys.

*Turkey vultures are found year round in the southernmost part of their range near the Falkland Islands.*

After the last space shuttle launched in 2011, vultures were left to share the skies with NASA's experimental rockets.

Turkey vultures are captured, named, and fitted with GPS tracking devices. Visitors to the project's Web site can monitor the vultures along with the researchers.

Even the National Aeronautics and Space Administration (NASA) is now researching vultures, particularly turkey and black vultures, whose droppings litter bleachers and walkways at the Kennedy Space Center in Florida. The birds also have a history of getting in the way of space shuttle liftoffs and landings. Wing tags and GPS devices are employed to study vulture movements, behavior patterns, and habitat range. NASA will not try to rid the area of vultures; rather, it hopes to learn how to coexist with the vultures in ways that are safer for both humans and the birds.

Vultures are amazing birds that fulfill a vital role in the life cycle of their **ecosystems** by helping maintain the natural process of decay and cleanup. It is important for people who share vulture habitats to respect and manage both human and wildlife activities in order to sustain healthy environments that protect vultures from the hazards they too often face. It is up to us to give them a certain—and safer—future.

In 1973, the world's highest-flying bird, a Rüppell's griffon vulture, collided with an airplane flying 36,100 feet (11,000 m) above the ground.

# ANIMAL TALE: THE VULTURE'S SACRIFICE

**Many American Indians believe that animals helped shape the world. The following Cherokee myth about the role the vulture played in the formation of the land reveals the close ties that they believe bind all native peoples to the vulture and cause them to respect its place in the world.**

Long ago, Earth was covered with water, and all the animals and birds lived above the rainbow in the sky, where they were very crowded. Water Beetle helped make land, but it was muddy and soft.

"When the mud hardens," Water Beetle told the other animals, "you can live on the land."

The animals sent Chickadee to check on the ground. "It is still too soft," he reported. "There is no place for me to land."

Later, they sent Crow, but he came back with the same news: "It is still too soft."

For many years, all the birds took turns flying down to the earth, and all found it too muddy and soft to land. Finally, they asked Grandfather Buzzard to fly down and check the land. He was heavy and flew close to the earth, which was still soft, and the wind created by his great wings began to dry the mud. He flew all around, hardening the land.

Soon, though, he grew tired and drifted closer to the earth. With each downward stroke, Grandfather Buzzard's wings touched the mud and tore deep valleys in the land. With each upsweep of his wings, he created high mountains out of the mud. Soon the land was dry and solid—and it was marked with mountains, ridges, hills, and valleys.

Delighted with the variety of landscapes from which to choose for their homes, all the animals joined Grandfather Buzzard on Earth. But it was too hot there. The sun, fascinated by Grandfather Buzzard's work, had followed him down from the sky and now sat too close to the land. The animals sent Chickadee to push the sun away from Earth, but Chickadee burned the top of his head before reaching the sun and had to give up. That is why his head is black on top.

Next, the animals sent Crow to push the sun away. Crow got closer to the sun, but he felt his whole body being scorched before he reached the sun and had to give up as well. That is why his entire body is black.

Finally, the animals asked Grandfather Buzzard to push the sun away from the Earth. Grandfather Buzzard flew high into the sky. As he approached the sun, he could feel the heat begin to scorch his head. Still, he kept going. Then he could feel the heat begin to scorch his body. Still, he kept going.

Soon he reached the sun and, using his head, began pushing the sun away from Earth. The heat was unbearable, but Grandfather Buzzard pushed and pushed, flapping his wings furiously. Soon the sun was far from Earth, and Grandfather Buzzard returned home.

When the animals saw Grandfather Buzzard, they were saddened. His body and wings were scorched black, and all the feathers on his head were burned off. To repay him for his sacrifice, the animals all agreed to give themselves to Grandfather Buzzard.

"When we die," the animals promised, "you will feast on our bodies." And so this has been the way of things since the days of long ago.

## GLOSSARY

**captive-rearing** – raising offspring in a place from which escape is not possible

**carrion** – the rotting flesh of an animal

**coat of arms** – the official symbol of a family, state, nation, or other group

**contaminated** – negatively affected by exposure to a polluting substance

**ecosystems** – communities of organisms that live together in environments

**egg tooth** – a hard, toothlike tip of a young bird's beak or a young reptile's mouth, used only for breaking through its egg

**evolved** – gradually developed into a new form

**extinction** – the act or process of becoming extinct; coming to an end or dying out

**Global Positioning System** – a system of satellites, computers, and other electronic devices that work together to determine the location of objects or living things that carry a trackable device

**indigenous** – originating in a particular region or country

**mythology** – a collection of myths, or popular, traditional beliefs or stories that explain how something came to be or that are associated with a person or object

**Neolithic** – a period in human history characterized by the use of stone tools and the beginning of farming

**nuisance** – something annoying or harmful to people or the land

**plumage** – the entire feathery covering of a bird

**pupil** – the dark, circular opening in the center of the eye through which light passes

**satellite** – a mechanical device launched into space; it may be designed to travel around Earth or toward other planets or the sun

**warm-blooded** – maintaining a relatively constant body temperature that is usually warmer than the surroundings

## SELECTED BIBLIOGRAPHY

Animal Planet. "Condor." http://animal.discovery.com/birds/condor/.

Dunne, Pete. *The Wind Masters: The Lives of North American Birds of Prey.* New York: Mariner Books, 2003.

Houston, David. *Condors and Vultures.* Minneapolis: Voyageur Press, 2001.

The Peregrine Fund. "Vultures." http://www.peregrinefund.org/explore_raptors/vultures/vultmain.html.

San Diego Zoo. "Animal Bytes: Vultures." http://www.sandiegozoo.org/animalbytes/t-vulture.html.

Weidensaul, Scott. *The Raptor Almanac: A Comprehensive Guide to Eagles, Hawks, Falcons, and Vultures.* Guilford, Conn.: Lyons Press, 2004.

*Turkey vultures often watch as farmers plow fields, ready to clean up any small animals that fall victim to the equipment.*

## INDEX